101 people were killed in the Wallsend Colliery disaster, of whom 76 were young boys. The death of nearly half the workforce was devastating; almost every family in the community was affected. And yet this explosion was just one of 11 serious explosions at the colliery in 53 years. Mining has always been a notoriously dangerous industry: since the opening of the first coal mine in the UK in 1575, thousands of miners have died in gas explosions, roof cave-ins and flooding. Sir Humphry Davy's invention of the safety lamp in 1815 did reduce the numbers of underground explosions and gassings, but even as recently as 2011, four miners were killed in a mine in Wales.

The last pit at Wallsend Colliery was closed in 1935, and the last deep pit mine in the UK closed in 2015.

The books in "Found on the Shelves" have been chosen to give a fascinating insight into the treasures that can be found while browsing in The London Library. Now celebrating its 175th anniversary, with over seventeen miles of shelving and more than a million books, The London Library has become an unrivalled archive of the modes, manners and thoughts of each generation which has helped to form it.

From essays on sherry and claret to a passionate defence of early air travel, from advice on how best to navigate the Victorian dinner party to accounts of European adventures, they are as readable and relevant today as they were more than a century ago—even if small boys are no longer permitted to work in coal mines.

A FULL ACCOUNT OF THE DREADFUL EXPLOSION OF WALLSEND COLLIERY, BY WHICH 101 HUMAN BEINGS PERISHED!

The London Library

Pushkin Press

Pushkin Press
71–75 Shelton Street,
London WC2H 9JQ

*A Full Account of the Dreadful Explosion of Wallsend Colliery, by
which 101 Human Beings perished! And four others were severely
injured. – The Names of the Sufferers and Survivors, and various
Particulars of the unfortunate Families. – The 5 Days' Inquest, and
Examination of all the Witnesses – The Names of the Jury, and their
Verdict. – Particulars of the Funerals, and the Customs of the Pitmen
on such Occasions. – With an Account of Mr R. Ayre's improved Safety
Lamp.* Newcastle: Printed and sold by W. Fordyce, [1835?]

"Sketch of a Wallsend Colliery, 1840" and "Old North of England
Colliery", published in R. Nelson Boyd, *Coal Pits and Pitmen*. London:
Whittaker & Co., 1895

"Air Shaft, Wallsend" and "The Church Pit, Wallsend" by Thomas
Harrison Hair (1808–1875), published in Madeleine Hope Dodds, *A
History of Northumberland*. Newcastle-Upon-Tyne: Andrew Reid &
Co., 1930

First published by Pushkin Press in 2016

9 8 7 6 5 4 3 2 1

ISBN 978 1 782273 25 7

Set in Goudy Modern by Tetragon, London

Printed by CPI Group (UK) Ltd, Croydon, CR0 4YY

www.pushkinpress.com

EXPLOSION, &C.

A colliery explosion, more disastrous than any that can be remembered by the oldest inhabitant of this district, or probably that ever before occurred, took place on Thursday afternoon, the 18th June, 1835, at one of Mr. Russell's coal mines, situated at Wallsend, about four miles east of Newcastle. By this dreadful accident one hundred and one of our fellow creatures were suddenly hurried into eternity, and four others severely injured. Every particular connected with so melancholy an accident must be interesting to hundreds in this district; and though this has been given most minutely in the public papers at the time, yet it is thought the same will be more acceptable to many in a pamphlet form, and without further observation we will proceed to a full and minute detail of the whole affair.

Sketch of a Wallsend Colliery, 1840.
A: funnel over upcast shaft; B: smoke dispenser;
C: platform for repairs; D: head gear;
E: engine house; F: counterpoise

In working a coal mine it is necessary to sink pits or shafts, and in the above mine three are sunk; they are at considerable distances from each other, but have internal communications. One of them is situated near to Wallsend Church, not far from the banks of the river Tyne. It is known as the "Church Pit," or "Russell's Old Wallsend." It is the practice at this, as at other collieries, for the "hewers" of the coal to commence working early in the morning, and having finished their labours for the day, the "putters" remain for some time longer, for the purpose of bringing or "putting" the coal to the bottom of the shaft or pit, that it may be raised from the mine to the bank. Altogether about 250 people are employed at this colliery, and on Thursday afternoon the hewers of the coal, with the exception of four, had left the mine, under an impression of its perfect safety. About 100 putters, consisting for the most part of young men and boys remained at work. While the operation of "putting" the coals was going on, the banksmen were suddenly alarmed by a loud report in the Church Pit, which they describe as being similar to an earthquake. The rushing of the foul air to the mouth of the shaft, bringing up with it some of the pitmen's clothes and other light articles from the bottom, left no room for conjecture as to what had occurred in the mine.

To those unacquainted with the arrangements of Northern coal mines, it may be necessary to state that the workmen of each colliery form, with their families, a distinct colony. They are provided with cottages, forming long streets, near the works. Amongst the community resident near the mine in question, intelligence of the explosion

Old North of England Colliery

spread with the utmost rapidity. The distressing scene that ensued no pen can describe. Parents, wives, and children rushed to the pit, eager to ascertain the extent of the calamity, and the fate of those who were near and dear to them. Eight brave men, notwithstanding the imminent risk and danger of such an experiment, volunteered to descend the pit, in the desperate hope of being able to save and bring up some of their companions. On reaching the bottom, and endeavouring to penetrate the works, they were nearly suffocated by the foul air. With the greatest difficulty they regained the ropes, and when drawn up were nearly insensible and in a state of extreme exhaustion. Thus perished all hopes of saving any of the unfortunate people in the mine, and of the large assemblage collected, there was scarcely an individual but had to mourn the sudden bereavement of some beloved relative. During the following day (Friday) 21 of the bodies were brought up—they were obtained by descending one of the other shafts of the mine, it being yet impossible to enter Church Pit. The bodies were removed to the houses of their respective friends, and the entire community of the colliery was in a state of the most dreadful agitation and distress. Several of the bodies were black, shrivelled, and burnt; one or two were mutilated, but the greater portion, having been suffocated by the after damp, had the appearance of being in a tranquil sleep.

On Friday evening at 8 o'clock, a jury was summoned to attend the office of John Buddle, Esq. the head-viewer, or professional conductor of the mine. The following gentlemen were then sworn—A. Easterby, Esq. foreman; Rev. J. Armstrong, vicar of Wallsend; Messrs. J. Wright, W. Potts, J. Falcus, P. Pye, W. Jamieson, R. H. Coward, M. Elliott, J. Mordue, G. Brough, G. Shanks, and C. Weatherley. [Three other

Air Shaft, Wallsend.

gentlemen were also on the jury, but being connected by relationship with parties interested
in the inquiry, it was thought prudent, at the
adjourned inquest, to withdraw their names.]
Stephen Reed, Esq. the coroner, then addressed
them. The cause of the accident, he observed,
would not probably be ascertained, for it most
unfortunately happened that in this, as well as in
most other similar calamities, the individuals who
were nearest the explosion were the first to suffer.
They would, however, hear the testimony of witnesses, whose scientific and practical knowledge
would probably enable them to draw correct and
proper conclusions. Their first duty, and a most
painful one it was, would be to view the bodies of
John Robson, and 20 other individuals, who had
lost their lives by this distressing accident. This
would enable him at once to issue his warrant for
the interment of the unfortunate sufferers, and
thus leave the survivors at liberty to perform the
last melancholy offices of humanity. The inquest
could then be adjourned to some convenient day,
when evidence, more satisfactory than could be
at present obtained, would probably be adduced.

A rigid and sifting inquiry would be necessary; for the frequency of accidents in mines, and the awful loss of life consequent thereon, had at length attracted the attention of the legislature, and a committee of the House of Commons was now sitting, with a view to investigate their cause, and if possible to provide a remedy.

The jury then went to the houses of the deceased to view the bodies. In one instance two brothers were laid on the same bed, and in another house lay, stretched side by side, the father and son. These scenes, accompanied as they were by mental agony and domestic sorrow, were truly heart rending. In almost every case the body was strewed with evergreens and flowers, and the parents, sisters, or brothers, weeping around the bed of death. The jury having performed the melancholy duty of viewing the bodies, the inquest was adjourned to Monday week, the 29th inst.

The excitement which existed in the neighbourhood of the mine, for several days, cannot easily be described. On Sunday last great crowds of people repaired to Wallsend, to witness the funerals of those whose bodies had been

The Church Pit, Wallsend

recovered, and visitors from all parts of the country have since been attracted to the spot. The interest attending this melancholy affair was considerably increased on Saturday night, when, on removing the materials at the bottom of the G Shaft, thrown down by the explosion, three men and a boy were brought up alive. The preservation of these individuals is miraculous. They had gone down the pit on the morning of Thursday, about 5 o'clock, and had thus been underground, at a depth of 145 fathoms for 65 hours—and as the explosion took place at 2 in the afternoon of Thursday, they had literally been entombed alive for 56 hours of the above period. Two of them when taken out were delirious, and gave incoherent and improbable accounts of what had transpired; another had his leg so fractured as to render immediate amputation indispensable; the fourth had his hands and face scorched, but was perfectly sensible, and is in a fair way of recovery; John Brown, the most intelligent of the survivors, states that he was at the bottom of the shaft of the G or Church Pit when the accident took place. He was what is called an "onsetter," his duty being to fix the hook at the end of the rope upon the corves of coals previous to their being drawn up from the mine. He says that he was in the act of performing this duty, when the pit "fired." The blast which came through the pit knocked him down, and he fell with his side upon the tram, or rolley, used for bringing the corves of coals. Near him was a little boy, Martin Delap, and at a short distance the other two men. How long Brown lay insensible he is not able to conjecture; but when he recovered sufficiently to reflect, he knew that a "blast" had occurred in the pit. The lights were, of course, "extinguished" by the foul air, and on groping about, the first thing that he discovered was, that the horse, within a few yards of him, had been killed, either by the blast of fire or the after damp. He eventually discovered the boy and the other two men. He got some water and refreshed himself and them. One of the men was already delirious; he talked of his wife and his home, and insisted upon stripping his clothes off, under an impression that he was going to bed. In that state he lay upon the floor of the mine, and the poor sufferers continued in this state of living death, until the happy hour of deliverance. The individuals thus miraculously preserved, do not appear to have suffered from hunger.

The greatest praise and gratitude is due to the pitmen belonging the colliery, and to many others from distant parts, for their laudable and humane exertions in descending the mine to recover the bodies of those who have perished. A gentleman present, on one of these occasions, describes the scene as one of deep and melancholy interest. In a shed near the G pit were several females, waiting in silent despair the result of those exertions about to be made to recover their relatives, and near them were a number of coffins. In another shed, still nearer the pit, a man was engaged in trimming, cleaning, locking, and lighting Davy lamps, to give light and security to the pitmen about to explore the mine. With these adventurous men, the shed and the space around the pit were crowded. The rain descended in torrents, but they heeded it not. All being in readiness, four men took their Davy lamps, and got into the corf. The signal was given, the machinery set in motion, and instantly they were out of sight. The operation was repeated until about 28 men had descended. There was no hesitation with any of them; the competition rather seemed to be, which should go down first. All was, however, conducted in silence, except the hoarse voice of the banksman giving the necessary signals. In about half an hour, a rush of the spectators to the pit mouth proclaimed that a body had been brought to bank. The women eagerly joined the throng, but instantly retired without a word—it was not he whom they sought, but a little boy named Appleby, of whom an interesting anecdote is told. The accident occurred in the race week, the day appointed for the cup to be run for. The deceased had finished his own work, but had bargained with another boy, who was anxious to visit the Race Course, to remain at work for him. The stipulated wages for this service was one shilling—that shilling cost the deceased his life.

On Monday, the entire vicinity of the mine presented an appearance indescribably agonizing. On the afternoon of that day, about 60 bodies were conveyed, in carts, to the parish church, where they were interred. It may not be

uninteresting to describe the ceremonies or customs, which preceded interment in each instance,
and which is usual throughout the pit districts,
when death has occurred; two young men go
round the neighbourhood, apprising the inhabit-
ants that such-a-one is dead, and requesting their
presence at the funeral at the time appointed. The
young men who perform this service are called
"askers." At the time appointed the people invited
proceed to the house of the deceased, dressed in
their holiday clothes, and sit down. On the table
is placed a cheese, and a supply of bread and ale.
Portions of these are handed to the visitors by
two young women, dressed in mourning, who
are called "servers," and it is not unusual for the
men to indulge in a pipe of tobacco in addition.
This custom is, however, observed in silence,
and with a solemnity and decorum befitting the
melancholy occasion. When all the visitors have
been "served," the coffin, containing the body,
is brought to the door, and placed upon chairs.
A hymn is then sung, after which it is borne to
the grave, preceded by the "askers," with black
scarfs over their dress, and the "servers" with

white hoods. After the body follow those who mourn for the deceased, and the attendants bring up the rear. In the present melancholy instance, as has been said, the bodies were taken to the graves in carts, but a black pall was, in each instance, thrown over the coffin. In some cases 3 were taken from one house, and the scenes of distress—the lamentation and woe—visible in every direction, it was impossible to view unmoved. The coffins were furnished by the owners of the mine, who also contributed £1, in addition, for the interment of each body.——There were in the mine, at the time of the explosion, 11 horses, all of which were killed.

In consequence of 60 other bodies having been recovered from the mine, as above stated, during Saturday and Sunday, the Coroner deemed it prudent to alter the previous arrangement of adjournment, and the jury was consequently summoned to attend at 4 o'clock, on the 22nd of June at Mr. Buddle's office. The jury having attended, it was proposed by Mr. Buddle to adjourn to the Wesleyan Chapel School House, in order to give an opportunity to as many of the work people as thought proper to attend, to hear the examination of witnesses. This suggestion being acquiesced in, Mr Buddle sent messengers to inform the workmen of the arrangement, and shortly after many were in attendance, who were informed that they would be allowed the privilege of putting questions to the witnesses. The Coroner then addressed the jury on the important duty they had to discharge, and hoped they would perform it without favour or partiality to any individual. Mr. Buddle was then called in, and exhibited a number of drawings and plans of the mine; he gave a very interesting statement as to the quantity of inflammable air which was perpetually evolved, and the methods adopted to ventilate the mine. It was suggested by a juryman that Mr. Buddle should be sworn, and his testimony taken in the regular way. This met with the approbation of the jury.

Mr. Buddle said, I have been a viewer, I am now almost sorry to say, 43 years. I have had the sole direction of this colliery since 1806. It had been wrought about 11 years before that time. The main coal-seam there was wrought wholly;

it was from 6 to 7 feet thick. The next was the metal coal-seam, only partially wrought; it was 3 feet thick; the succeeding one was the present Bensham seam, opened in 1821, and now in course of working. It may be called 5 feet 6, but it varies; it is interstratified by stone. The pit where the explosion happened is 152 fathoms. [Some doubt arose on this, and it was ascertained to be somewhere between 140 and 150 fathoms from the surface.] Though not a general principle, yet, in respect to Wallsend colliery, the deeper we go the more hydrogen gas we find. The workings extend to about 100 acres in the Bensham seam. The coals are only drawn from one shaft, the G pit; it is a double shaft, and the coals are drawn on both sides of the brattice. There are five ventilating shafts. They are to admit the atmospheric air and dispel the hydrogen; the atmospheric air descends down two, and comes up three; the former being the downcasts, and the latter the upcasts. The Bensham seam has always been considered as a very dangerous seam, and required the most critical management which we could devise, and, therefore, the most improved system

21

of ventilation has been adopted and pursued. I do not think that it would have been prudent to have put down more shafts; there is not a pit in the country that has such a number of ventilators. These five shafts have been found amply sufficient hitherto. From my experience I do not believe that this accident has arisen from any defect in the ventilation. As I have already stated, the seam is about 5 feet 6 from the roof to the pavement. There is a band runs through the seam about 2 feet 10 from the roof; it wedges from nothing up to 15 or 16 inches in these wallings. It is 16 inches thick at the west, and it nearly disappears to the eastward. The men work in different districts for the purpose of dividing the risk, so that if an explosion should take place in one district, it might not extend to another. The nearest division was working full 500 yards from the shaft of the G pit, where the explosion took place, which was the most dangerous part of the pit. This particular part was at the extremity of our east boundary, and as the coal was wrought away, the roof naturally fell in, there being no pillars left to support it. It then becomes a *goaf*, or void, and consequently a very great quantity of foul air lodges there. At these situations the circulation of air is carried in the face of the void, to carry off the quantity of air emitted from the *goaf*, or void, into the gas drift, by which it is carried into the upcast pit, (which is 2000 yards from where the foulness comes from) and discharged without being allowed to come into contact with the furnace, which is used for the purpose of rarefaction. At another broken working, similar to the last, there was a party working at the distance of upwards of one thousand yards from the shaft of the G pit, where the explosion took place. Both these parties were working in the pillars. Another party were working in the whole mine (where the coal is not wrought before) at the same distance as the last, and the fourth party was working at about nine hundred yards (also in the whole mine) from the G shaft. In all these workings inflammable air exists, and wherever it does exist, it is carried off into the gas drifts in a distinct and separate current of air in the pillar workings, whilst the inflammable air from the whole workings is carried off by its appropriate current to the furnaces in the upcast shafts. I have been down since, and I could form no idea of the cause. In all the currents where they were working in the pillared divisions, they were working with Davy lamps; where they were working the whole coal they were using candles. But wherever, even in the whole coal, it is dangerous, candles are withdrawn, and the Davy lamps used. In the vicinity of one of the divisions where the whole coal was worked, there was also a division of men working in pillars. The places might be distant one hundred yards, and were properly divided by a course of substantial air-stoppings, by which the currents of air already described were kept separate and independent of each other. If any of those stoppages were injured, I would apprehend no danger. No serious danger would occur, as the current of fresh-air would preponderate, and pass off with the adulterated current. I was down these pits three weeks previous to the accident, but I cannot say exactly. I only make occasional visits. I then found every thing in order—the system of ventilation was in good order in all its details.—I go down voluntarily, for my own satisfaction;

it is not my duty to go down the Wallsend pit,
yet for my own satisfaction I take an occasional
inspection. The daily details and inspection of the
colliery are entrusted to Mr. John Atkinson, the
viewer, his overman, deputy overman, and other
assistants. He takes whom he finds necessary for
his purpose, who are daily down; in fact, there is
a regular system, and every man that has charge
is a tried good man, and has been promoted by
merit. I was down on Friday morning, but I could
not from any observation ascertain the cause. My
object was to see what was best to be done. The
first body I came to was that of the deputy-overman; and that was as far as could be got with
safety at that time. The deputy had been at his
post, and had crept a small distance. He was no
way burnt; his name was Robson. He must have
died of suffocation, from the explosion having
deranged the ventilation. The next thing was to
get the pit ventilated, and I sent to Mr. Johnson
and others. The pit was not much destroyed
where I went in. As far as we have been able to
explore there are no indications to show where
the explosion first took place, but we have every

reason to think that it did not take place in any of the working divisions.——The reason that candles are used in working the whole coal is, that it is necessary to work the coal with gunpowder by blasting the powder. These blasts are chiefly by the hewers, and there were then six down when this took place; but I consider those little blasts as preventing the great ones; they could not be used at all if the ventilation was not perfect; they are a test of the healthy ventilation of the mine. [The coroner here said it would be impossible to finish the investigation this evening, he would therefore adjourn the inquest until the next day at 12 o'clock.]

Tuesday, June 23. This morning Mr. Buddle was again examined. I have already observed that the Bensham seam abounds with inflammable air. In order that an idea may be formed of the quantity discharged, I take, for example, the quantity which is now in a state of combustion at the top of the gas-pipe of the C pit. This stream of gas issues from a detached portion of the workings of about 5 acres in area, the quantity as gauged issuing from that pipe is eleven hogsheads per minute.

Supposing this feeder of gas were suffered to pass through the workings, it would require from 150 to 160 hogsheads of atmospheric air per minute to dilute it below the firing point, so as to allow it to be carried through the firable points. I consider the three downcast shafts are amply sufficient to convey a sufficient quantity of air to render the workings safe. But the working in the broken, or pillars, is absolutely dangerous, and cannot be worked without the aid of the Davy lamp. About 750 yards from the broken, and 150 yards to the east of the G pit, there are some old workings which have fallen in; and to prevent the workmen having access to these old workings, they are built up with strong stoppings, excepting two doors for the access of the wastemen, whose business is to travel the gas-pipe, or dumb drift, for the purpose of keeping it free and open at all times, which doors are kept constantly locked, except when the wastemen have occasion to go through them. These places are never entered without a safety-lamp. In 1821, when the Bensham seam was first opened, the dangerous nature of the seam was soon discovered from the fatal accident which took place on the 21st of October in that year, showed the necessity of adopting the most efficient mode of ventilation which could be devised. At that time only one pit was sunk to this seam, the workings were therefore suspended until other pits were sunk, and progressively five in all were sunk to this seam, as already stated, and the present system of ventilation brought to its now improved state.

John Atkinson said—I live at Wallsend. I am an under viewer there. I have been in that situation three years and a half; my duty is to see that all the workings are kept in proper order. I am down nearly every day, sometimes twice a day. I came up on Thursday morning about half-past seven o'clock; at that time as far as I could discover every thing was safe, and the currents of air free and good. The Bensham seam, particularly in the brokens, makes a good deal of gas; generally the pit is safe to work in. We can work the broken well enough with the Davy lamp, if no misfortune happens. On Thursday morning the pit was in a particularly good working state; I was round all the working part of it. It was perfectly safe when

I left it. Shortly before the accident, which was about half past two o'clock, all the hewers had come up but six. About 88 had left, but I cannot say to a man. The occasion of the six men remaining was, that they went in when the others left. They remained, not having finished their work. They were working the whole coal in the north division. Two of them were near the extremity at the north-west district, and the other four within 200 yards of them. These men were working with candles. The mine there was sufficiently well ventilated to admit of it with safety. In going to the whole coal, they had not to pass any place where the pit would fire with a candle. The rolley way which they would pass is never in such a state as to fire with a candle. It proceeds in a direct line near to the quarter where they had to work. It is at the face of the boards when they are drilling the holes to blast the coal, the gas sometimes fires, but that is in such small quantities that it is soon dashed out by an old jacket or piece of blanket. If they were not active in dashing it out, it would fire the coal when they took out their stones, but it would not communicate with the other parts of the mine. I have been near where the men were working; there is nothing but after damp; the mine is not much hurt. As far as I have been able to explore, the accident did not happen there. We have been prevented going in for want of air, not by rubbish. The board is about 8 inches thick there. I visited the broken, in the 4th district of the C pit the same morning. I went down the Church pit, and was down 6 hours. The men had Davys. The foul air was not bad there. It sometimes fires at a lamp in the gas drift. There has been no wastemen through the drift that morning. The board is about 8 inches thick there. The pitmen have to separate the stone from the coal before it comes to bank. They are fined 6d. a corf when stone is found, and more as the quantity increases. They are liable to pay from 6d. to 2s. 6d. If there is an extra quantity, the coals are forfeited altogether. It is natural they should like as much light to select the coal as possible, but the Davy gives plenty of light for that, though they cannot do it very expeditiously. I never, in my experience at Wallsend, knew of their taking off their Davy-top for the purpose of their work. Our lamps are all locked. I have heard tell of it being done at other places, and for the purpose of lighting their pipes. They can light their pipes at the gause by drawing the flame to the wire. The mine may not be in a bad state at the time. When such an occurrence has come to the knowledge of the viewer, the men have been invariably displaced. At the north-east part of the mine, west of the G pit-shaft, the waste-men and I had travelled the gas-drift on Thursday morning, from near the broken at the north-east, next the barrier to the west of the G pit-shaft, which would be about 600 yards. I found the drift in a very good state; it would then be between three and four o'clock. I call it in a good state when it will not fire at a lamp. I have known the drift fire at a lamp in the C pit, but not in this one. I left it at the G shaft, and came through the wood doors there. We locked the doors behind us. We lost a lock between six and seven months ago. It has occurred 3 times since I have been at Wallsend. I have known three taken off in one week. It would be dangerous to have these doors thrown open. They are now all blown away; but nothing material has happened in consequence that we know of. I have frequently known the men smoke in the whole boards, but that is not dangerous there. There are none allowed in the broken quarters; if they are known to do so there the men are discharged on account of the danger. I never knew a workman go into the waste through those doors.

By the Rev. Mr. Armstrong——None of the men have complained to me of the state of the mine. The Davy fired at the broken the day before, but that is not an unusual occurrence.

By the Foreman.——The band is 2 feet 10 inches, but it varies.

John Atkinson, jun.——I am son to the last witness. I am overman in this colliery. I have been employed there three years.——My duty is to go down the pit every day, and see that every thing is right; if there be any particular part which I cannot see, or don't think neces-sary to see, I take the report from my deputies. We have two deputies in the fore shift. They are there the whole of the time during which the men are employed. There are six overmen and deputies in the establishment; a first and second overman and four deputies. I was down the pit a little after two on the morning of the accident; I found every thing right, and a little better than usual in some parts; we had a less discharge of gas that morning than usual—particularly than there was the morning before. This favourable state of the pit enabled me to go through three working districts of the pit out of the four. The reason for me not being through the fourth district was that my father and one of the wastemen went through, whilst I was at one of the others. I met them, and they asked if all was right, and I told them it was, and I went with them into the return, and found that it was clean upon the lamp. There had been some foulness there the morning before.—*Adjourned.*

Thursday, June 25.—The examination of Mr. Atkinson, jun., was then resumed—On entering the mine in the morning, his first visit was to the second north east district, which consists of the "broken" coal. This was before the "hewers" commenced, which would be about 3 o'clock, and the number appointed to work there would be about eighteen. His object in being there before the workmen was to ascertain if there was any superabundant discharge of gas. He was induced to do so from the circumstance of there having been an unusual emission of gas on the previous day, but which ceased in about half-an-hour or three-quarters. Each man has a Davy-lamp which is placed in a situation to give him light whilst working. The gas will not explode even if the Davy lamp remains in a state of flame; the wire-gauze of the lamp is red hot. There is always danger of an explosion when the props are withdrawn at the "broken," (or parts where the coal is worked out) to let down the stone. When performing this operation, the men have the "Davies" in their hands, and immediately retire to a considerable distance from the place of danger, and do not return until it is safe to do so. The old workings at the south-west of the G shaft form a complete gasometer, and if not for the judicious means adopted of carrying a fresh current of air round the skirt of the goaf, it would be totally unapproachable. There are "main-doors" in the course of the current of fresh air, for ventilating large portions of the mine, and various trap-doors for ventilating smaller portions, which, if negligently left open or accidently injured, would cause danger, by diverting the air currents from their course. The consequence would be to fill the workings with dangerous "foulness;" but there are two doors in each instance, so that if one is injured, the other would remain as a protection. The trap-doors are substitutes for permanent brick "stoppings." Has known one trap-door accidentally injured, and sometimes negligently left open—but never both. They are used for the ingress and egress of trams (a small cart), drawn by boys. Witness and his deputies examine these passages frequently each day. The trap-doors remain open, except in cases where the "hewers" require additional ventilation. The trap-doors are then closed, and boys or old and infirm men, but competent for that duty, called "trappers," are stationed to open and shut the doors when required. Has known a "trapper" leave his post, but not far. On those occasions the trappers have been reprimanded or punished; a repetition of the offence would cause their immediate dismissal. Great care is taken to place the younger boys in situations of the least danger; and the older boys and the men are placed in situations where the greatest care and attention is necessary. The old men have Is. 4d. per day, and the boys from 10d. to Is. 2d. At present the mine is worked, upon the average, about five days a week. But for the precautions taken to ventilate the mine, the workings of the Bensham Seam would be entirely unapproachable. About four o'clock on the morning of the accident, and after the men had commenced working out the "broken," witness entered the drift, called the "dumb" or "gas-drift," and ascertained that it was not sufficiently foul to inflame the air in the Davy-lamp. The healthy state of the atmosphere proved that all the doors, connected with that part of the pit, were properly secured. The currents of air are so directed as to carry out the gas at the south-west of the G shaft through the dumb-furnace, into the B pit shaft. The gas, so long as the air-mines are clear, cannot possibly escape into the workings. After satisfying himself with the safety and proper order of the second north-east district, and set the boys to work at their proper stations, he proceeded to the second north-west district, where men were working both broken and whole coal. There were eight men at the whole coal, and from fourteen to sixteen at the pillar-work, the distance between the two divisions being about 150 yards. Found the state of ventilation good in every respect. From the old workings in this part, there is an immense discharge of gas, which escapes into the C pit gas drift, the mine being kept clear where the men have to work by a sufficient current of air. The same observations as to main-doors, trap-doors, and air-courses, apply to this district as to that already described. There is no communication between the pillar-workings and the whole-workings in this quarter, except by the tram-road, which is nearly two hundred yards in length. The men work in what are called "boards" of two each—each board being twenty yards apart. At the whole-coal the men worked with candles. In going to their occupation with these naked lights, they pass, for a short distance, within twenty-yards of the gas-drift. In going the direct way to their work they cannot possibly come in contact with a stream of gas. In the whole workings the men often blast with gunpowder. Previous to blasting, the band of stone in the seam of coal is taken out. Two or three holes are then drilled in the coal, from three to four feet deep, in which the charge is inserted. There is, in these holes, an occasional slight escape of gas, from which no danger arises. Has known slight explosions in which men have been burnt—but no lives lost—by working with candles in the Bensham Seam. These accidents are occasioned by negligence of the men or boys. It very seldom happens that an explosion takes place by working with gunpowder, and witness never knew an accident from that cause. Sometimes the coal "fires" from the blasting with gunpowder, but it is easily extinguished with the men's jackets. No objection is made to the men smoking tobacco when working in the whole-coal, but never knew a man even so much as take a pipe, lighted or unlighted, into the pillar-workings. They are strictly prohibited from doing so. Has heard of men lighting their pipes at a Davy-lamp, but not at this colliery. Never knew a man take off the cap of his Davy at Wallsend Colliery to give more light, but has heard that such conduct is occasionally practised at other collieries. When inspecting the mine, witness travels with a candle in the whole-coal, and with a Davy in the broken. All the men and boys knew their route through the mine perfectly well. They could not get into any dangerous part of the mine, except by breaking off a lock, or going with a candle into the working parts of the broken.

By the Foreman.——It is his business to examine the air-courses daily, both on entering and leaving the mine. On the morning when this misfortune happened, found the ventilation of the mine in good order. The number of hewers down that morning would be about eighty-six, who would descend at two o'clock in the morning.

By Mr. Armstrong.——There are open oil lamps (or common lamps) placed in different parts of the rolley-way, to give light to the horses. The nearest open lamp to the old workings in one direction would be about 140 or 150 yards from the double-doors in each division of the mine. The witness added, the lamps are always kept in the fresh air before used.

By the Coroner.——The state of the atmosphere has a material effect upon the effusion of gas in the mine——the emission being much greater when the atmosphere is dense. From the same cause the air carried through the mine to ventilate the workings is not so pure. Does not think it possible that, on these occasions, an emission of gas from the old workings could come in contact with the flame of the oil lamp, at a distance of 140 yards.

By Mr. Wright——The deputies went through the mine, and visited each man's place previous to the hewers going to their work. They finished their work and left the mine between the hours of half-past ten and twelve in the forenoon. Two of them had not come up at the time of the blast and four other persons had gone down about nine in the morning, making six hewers in all remaining in the mine at the time of the accident. The "putters", "trappers," and others, consisting of old men and boys, went down the mine at about half-past four in the morning, and had not finished their work when the accident took place.

By Mr. Falcus.——None of the men complained to witness that the pit was in a bad state——not one.

By Mr. Armstrong.——No part of the workings have "holed" into any part of the waste. Witness has been in those parts of the mine where it has been reported such a circumstance has occurred, but it is not correct. They have not yet been able to ascertain where the explosion originated.

The Coroner complimented Mr. Atkinson on having given his evidence in a very straightforward and satisfactory manner.

John Moor——I live at Shiney Row, and am a deputy overman. I have been employed about 27 years down the pit here. My duty is to go down before the men to see that the pit is all clear, and in a workable state, as far as my particular rounds extend——On the morning of the 18th, I went down as usual, and found the workings as free from gas as at any other time which I have experienced. On that morning there was nothing in the state of the weather when I went down to cause my particular attention. I first visited the first west crane; that is in the whole coal quarter;

from thence I went to all the boards in that quarter. I then went to the east crane, on the other side of the pit, in the broken. Having got to this point, my duty for this day ceased: I came up at half past nine. I found no difference in the pit; the whole detail of the pit was in order as far as I went. Before I left the pit, and after I had gone my rounds, I repeated to the man who next succeeded me, that I found nothing strange in the pit more than usual. After the accident I went down the C pit to do all the good I could. I went as far as I could get, 400 yards or more, and then I could get no farther for the after damp. In those 400 yards there was a good deal of damage done; the doors and stoppings were all blown down. I have not been in since.

Edward Combie——I live at Carville. I am a deputy overman at Wallsend Colliery. I have been in that capacity 15 or 16 months. My duty is to go round the pit in the morning, and see that all things are in a workable state; that is, before the men go to work; and to prepare timber to secure the roof. On the morning of the 18th I went down in the morning at half past one, and found the pit in a regular safe workable state. I first proceeded to the far west part of the workings, from thence to the far east part of the workings, and then my work ceased for the day. I came up again at eight o'clock in the morning. When I was down, I found occasion to set timber to secure the roof in the broken both east and west parts of the mine. I found every place I visited as clear as usual. I have been down since, but only sixty yards from the shaft. I have attended to repairing the shaft. None of the men made any complaint to me. [This and the last witness are the only deputies remaining]

John Bell—I live at Wallsend. I am a hewer. I have wrought here 19 years gone April last. I was down on the 18th; I went down about a quarter past two in the morning; I came up a little before 11 in the forenoon. I was working in the east way in the broken in the C pit. When I went in the morning she was not so bad as I left her the day before. I used a Davy lamp. There were five with me, and we all had Davy lamps. The day before the misfortune took place the pit was in so dangerous a state, that we were obliged to come away. We extinguished our Davy lamps before leaving, except one man, who reduced his light as small as possible so as to allow us to find our clothes before leaving. Edw. Combie had previously left us to go to some other men on the other side of the Mothergate to warn them away. There are separation doors between the foul air and the fresh, one of which may be about 60 yards from the headway where we go in to work. The entire distance from the place where we were working may be about 136 yards. The other door is about 80 yards further on. At this last door, which may be eight yards from the headway where we were working, there is placed about two yards and a half from it an old lamp. I considered this lamp to be placed too near the separation doors, and desired one of the boys who kept the lamp, and is lost, to shift it further out by, as I was apprehensive that if any fall took place where we were working, that the gas would be forced out with such violence against the separation doors, as to force through them and explode at the oil. These doors were quite in order, except, I consider, they were too glib. They had not a sufficient fall to. I never considered the door next the broken to have a sufficient fall to. Was never afraid till the 17th, when there was a fall, or rather a crush, occurred. I never mentioned the situation of the door, or that the lamp was too near to the outermost door, to any of the overmen. On the 18th when I went to work, the lamp which I complained of was still there; it was not burning when I went to work, but it was so when I returned. I said on passing the boy who had charge of the lamp, that it ought not to be there. I have not been down since, but from what I have heard, I have reason to believe the pit did not fire there. I saw the overman, John Atkinson, jun., at the place where I was working on the morning of the 17th, having sent for him in consequence of apprehension of the stone coming down; the roof bearing heavily upon the props caused the bottom to lift, and a quantity of gas escaped. The gas which came away was so overpowering, that we had to extinguish our Davys, as mentioned. On the overman arriving, I pointed out the stone. He said, if she came heavier in (more likely to fall) I was to take up the plates. About 4 or 5 hours after this the stone did fall, and the consequence was, the gas was forced out a great distance from the broken wall. The lamps then became red hot, and we extinguished them as soon as possible, and came away immediately. The deputy, Combie, was present when the stone fell, and left as before mentioned. The men who were working with me on the 17th were Charles Swan and Matt Buddle; we were working on the west side, and on the east side were T. Rutherford, Thos. Wilkinson, and Jacob Maddison. On the 18th that place was a great deal better, or we could not have gone in. There was a little fall on the 18th, but it did not prevent the men from doing their work. We left our work a quarter before 11, but we could not say the pit was then in a safe state for working. This was mentioned amongst the men, and to Joseph Lawson, who was a deputy, and a very cautious man, whom I told to be cautious. We left on the 18th not on account of the danger, but because our shift was finished. I believe that every one of the 6 lamps were on fire.

Thomas Rutherford, a hewer at Wallsend colliery, corroborated the last witness as to what happened on the 17th, and on the 18th, the day of the misfortune, he spoke to feeling extremely warm, and thought they had little air. He was not aware that his lamp had fired, but he was told those of other two had. When the boys came to fill the coals he told them to be cautious, for he had heard that some of the lamps had fired that morning. He does not think that the pit was warmer when he left than when he went in the morning. He never found the pit in so bad a state as it was after the fall on the 17th.

Charles Swan, hewer, had worked 14 years in the colliery, and 4 year in the Bensham seam, and always considered it dangerous to work in from the great quantity of foul air in it. On June 18, he was working in the broken, in the east part of the colliery, with the two last witnesses and Matthew Buddle. When he commenced work he placed the Davy as near the roof as he could get it, and it was fired immediately. He took it down and cautioned the other men. He put it up again and it fired. In attempting to fix it against a prop, it went out. He then sent it away by a putter to be lighted, but not till it was examined by the boy in charge—he got his lamp again, and continued to work till he was done. When he left he did not consider that part safe; the foul air was coming off the goaf at the north side of them. He left about half past ten: there was no fall the next day to his recollection. He told Simpson the back overman to caution the boys to be careful with the Davys; he did not say he considered the pit unsafe. James Hepple, the man who has the full charge of the Davy, never came near. The doors were all correct as far as he could judge. At best, with all the care which can be taken, he thinks the Bensham seam dangerous to work in. The men do not get higher wages for working in these dangerous places.

George Jude, aged 27, employed at Wallsend. For the last five days previous to the misfortune, he had been working in the whole coal; they worked with candles: the pit was well ventilated where he was. When they blasted the coal, there were no signs of fire. There was no old waste near them—he always considered the Bensham seam dangerous; believes that since the accident in 1821 the workings have been better ventilated.

Alex. Haxon, lives at the Long Row End, is a wasteman, and has been employed 23 years.

His duty is to keep the air waste good; is down seven hours per day. The Bensham seam is a more dangerous pit than any in this neighbourhood, and requires the utmost caution and attention to keep her in a workable state. On the 18th, John Atkinson and witness travelled all round the waste. The air was going on as good as ever they had it in their recollection. Went down before two in the morning, and came up about eight. Never heard any complaints from the men. Has heard them say their lamps were rather fiery, but it went off in about ten minutes. Cannot judge where the explosion commenced. There has been considerable damage done, especially in the first north-west division.

George Watkin, hewer, at Wallsend colliery, had been all his life there. Has worked in the whole coal seam, and has sometimes heard the workmen complain of too much air.

James Heppell has the inspection of the Davy Lamps at Wallsend Colliery. Never observed that the lamps had sustained injury, by widening the apartures of the wire. Has never known the locks interfered with. His duty is to clean the lamps, supply them with fresh cotton and oil, and lock them. Charles Swan was employed at the broken at the east crane. It was no part of witness's duty to visit that part. He gets the lamp safe from witness between two and three o'clock, and witness had two boys under him for the purpose of fetching the lamps from the "broken," which they retrim, light, and send back. Both the boys were lost.

Jacob Maddison is a hewer, has worked in the Bensham seam for several years. She is more dangerous than the Main Seam; but witness has no apprehension in working in the mine. Was working with John Bell and four other men in the "broken" on the 17th and 18th of June. (The witness here corroborated the other witnesses as to the state of the workings on the 17th and proceeded.) On the 18th, he was working back to back with John Bell, and witness's Davy did not fire, nor did he see any other lamp fire. He observed to his partner, when his shift came round, "the pit has behaved vary canny to-day;" and thought he had never wrought a pleasanter day's work. The pit was in a very workable state.

Charles Swan was working between 10 and 12 yards of witness. Has seen the mine in as bad a state as it was on the 17th, on one or two other occasions; it was caused in each instance by a fall. In one instance the Davy lamps fired.

John Dawson lives at Swan-row. Is a hewer, and has been employed at the colliery for 30 years. Has worked in the Bensham Seam seven or eight years. Considers it to be a very dangerous seam. Has known partial explosions of gas take place there, but no person injured, except on occasion of the two heavy misfortunes. Has known, in the East Narrow Broads where the coal is now working, the men be provided with wet cloths round a stick, to DOUSE out the fire. Remembers, on the second day after he went into the East Judds to work, seeing the lamps in such a state that he thought they should not be continued there. Went and sought the deputy, and told him. The deputy instantly appointed a "trapper" to a door, which made it safer to work by the admission of fresh air. (Adjourned.)

Monday, June 29 .—James Mc.Intyre, Esq. is surgeon to this colliery—had examined several of the bodies brought up from the mine. Some were exceedingly scorched with the fire, while others had no marks upon them—in his opinion they died of suffocation, by inhaling the carbonic acid gas.

Robert Giles and *Robert Usher* live at Wallsend, and are hewers at the Colliery. Were working at the broken seam on the 17th and 18th and did not observe any thing wrong. There was no "fall" of stone, and the ventilation was as usual.

Mr. John Atkinson, senr. under viewer was again examined. The furnace for ventilating is about 23 yards from the shaft bottom, at both the A and B pits. The gas is conveyed up the shaft about four fathoms above the furnace. It cannot come in contact with the flame. I have never known the gas fire at the furnace of the B pit. Two years and a half ago, a man was killed by an explosion of gas at the C pit. It was at the furnace where it happened, and the gas, in all probability, did fire there. It has not been burning since. A new furnace was built at the B pit—it was shifted further back as a precaution. The witness stated that they had been employed in heightening a drift—explained the manner of blasting the stone from the roof, and entered into a minute description of the situation of the main door and tramway main door, which are placed between the old workings or waste. The doors were not locked but have a sneck upon them. I consider it would be dangerous if those doors had been left open; it is possible if these doors were open the gas might fire at the candles the men had who were working at the rolley-way.

Robt. Moralee, one of the men who have been saved, was keeping a trap-door, about 60 yards west of the shaft of the G pit. The place where the two men were working at the rolley-way was from 300 to 350 yards to the west of where Morallee was tending the trap-door. (The foreman and the Rev Mr. Armstrong then detailed to the coroner the substance of the examination of Morallee and Delap. Morallee, who is unable to attend the court, said to them that the sensations he experienced at the time this accident must have taken place, was a ringing in his ears, and then he heard what he describes as a "booming" noise proceeding from the west; and then, immediately, he felt the door he was attending thrown against him. He was deprived of sensation, and when he recovered, he found what he thought to be the door lying upon him. They also examined John Middleton, a boy, who describes himself as being engaged on the west rolley-way. The first indication he had of something having gone wrong was a noise at the trap-doors to the west. This boy's account appears to coincide with Morallee's, but he is exceedingly ill, and unable to undergo much examination.)

John Atkinson, jun. re-examined. I was in the workings, in both quarters, on the morning of the 18th. There were two men working at the rolley-way increasing the height to admit of horses. The general height of the rolley-way is 6 feet 4 inches.

Alexander Haxon re-examined—was down in the workings on the 18th. Saw the doors where the men were working. Went through to examine the air. The doors are never locked. I have seen the men twice put their gear between the doors—I told them to put no more there, which they promised to observe. I put a lock on those doors, and on the 18th found them locked, and left them so after passing through.

By the *Rev. Mr. Armstrong*—The reason why the doors were not locked, was that they were considered so far out of the way both of the boys and men. I cannot say that these men left their gear between the two doors last spoken of, but I think it looks very like it.

Thomas Kennedy, Wallsend, furnace-keeper. Has been employed at this colliery nearly 40 years. My duty is to attend the furnace at the B pit. This furnace is at the bottom of the shaft. On the 18th I went down the G Pit. From the bottom of the shaft to the furnace will be nigh three quarters of a mile. I went along the drift which proceeds westward from the G Pit to the furnace. On my road I passed the place where two men were working at the roof of the drift, increasing the height of it to admit of a horse travelling along. These men were lighted at their work by candles. I never saw any men at this place with pipes. At the time when the explosion took place, I was convinced something wrong had happened from the current of air which was forced upon me. After remaining about a quarter of an hour, I, with my companion thought it prudent to leave the pit. We had great difficulty in escaping to the C pit.

James Patterson, Wallsend, banksman. Has been 40 years at this colliery. About 2 o'clock in the afternoon of the 18th June, and when employed at the shaft, a blast came up with such violence as threw an empty corf out of the shaft, and took his hat away over the pulley, about 26 feet from the ground. The shaft was immediately closed up with rubbish. When he looked at the C pit near Wallsend village, he saw the smoke coming out of it.

This closed the evidence on this melancholy affair, and the Coroner addressed the jury at considerable length, by recapitulating the evidence which we have already given. The jury, after deliberating about 20 minutes, gave the following verdict—"accidental death, arising from an explosion of inflammable air, but how, or in what part of the mine it originated, there is no evidence to show. In recording this verdict, the jury must express their full conviction that there has been no want of due care and precaution on the part of those who have the direction and management of the mine."

List of the Sufferers

IN THE LONG ROW——William Thompson, left a widow and five children——John Crozier, left a widow and two children. John, Percival, and John Reed, father and sons. John English, Roger Sharp, Hutton Rate, Edward and Robt. Combie, Robt. Wilkinson, Edw. Bell, Thos. Sharp, and James Cousin, all young men. Christopher Rate. James Thompson, George Kennedy, James and Edw. Combie, Wm. and David Patrick, Thomas Dawson, Wm. Wilkinson, John and Thos. Miller, Francis Haxon, Luke Watson, Ralph Waggot, John Christopher Waggott, all boys.

In Shiney Row——Ralph Waggot, an old man. Matthew Soulsby, onsetter, left a widow and three children. Wm. Johnson, left a widow and two children. Thomas and John Reaveley, father and son. James Green, John Chicken,

Henry Mackey, and Joseph Wright, young men. John Mason, John and Thomas Soulsby, Jas. and Thomas Moore, boys, brothers.

In Colliery Row.—Thomas Simpson, overman, and Josiah Harbottle, an old man. Wm, Craister, deputy overman. Wm. Craister, father and son. Francis, Richard, Wm. and Robt. Bell, brothers. John, Michael, and Matthew Buddle, brothers. John Stanners, a young man. Thos. Swan, Ralph Pendleton, Thomas Ellerton, and Henry and James Appleby, all boys.

In the West Row—Joseph Lawson, deputy overman, an old man. Andrew Reay, left a widow and 3 children. John Waggot, David Collins, and Wm. Reay, young men. Joseph Waniess, George Kyle, Thomas Huggup, and John and George Hall, all boys.

Swan's Row—Cuthbert, John, and Thomas Reveley, father and sons. Henry, John, and Andrew Giles, young men, brothers; John Gillis, young man. Joseph and Christopher Roseby, brothers. John and Joseph Roseby, brothers, and cousins to the above. Robert Roseby, John Heppel, and John Lowrey, all boys.

In Church Pit Row,——Christopher and Christopher Ovington, father and son. Martin Brown and Robert Clark, brothers-in-law, young men. Wm. and Bateman Dinning, boys, brothers.

In Bog Row——Luke, William, Peter, and Robt. Mason, brothers. James Miler, a young man.

In Twice-baked Row——John Brown, a widower, left a young orphan family. Peter Green, relative, residing with the above. John Thompson and Matthew Usher, boys.

In Wallsend Pit Row——John Robson, deputy-overman, and Andrew his son. John Robson has left a small family.

TAKEN OUT ALIVE. John Reed. Lies in a dangerous state, it being found necessary to amputate his leg.——*Now dead.*

John Brown, face and hands much scorched, but doing well, and likely to recover. He has a wife and small family.

Robert Moralee, a very old man, still in a dangerous state.

Martin Delap, a boy, doing well.

Summary

Total number of men and boys dead	101
Taken out alive	4
	105
Women deprived of their husbands	17
Widowed mothers deprived of their sons	7
Number of children under the age of 14 left fatherless	83
Total left unprovided for	107

Mr. R. Ayre's Safety Lamp

Connected with the present publication, we think a notice of an improvement of Sir Humphrey Davy's Lamp, now in use in our coal mines, will be interesting to the reader; more especially when we can state, that it is the opinion of those scientific gentlemen who have examined it, that its introducton into coal mines will completely prevent a recurrence of such dreadful accidents as above related. The lamp is shaped much similar to the Davy lamp, and its advantage consists in having an extinguisher suspended upon a thin

wire, near the top of the inside of the lamp. When
the gauze wire or lamp becomes heated, the wire
immediately straightens and yields its hold of the
extinguisher, and the light consequently put out.
The lamp is also so continued, that whenever the
pitmen endeavour to open it, either at the top
or the bottom, the extinguisher is in either case
dropped upon the light. In the case of the top, the
lid straightens the wire; in that of the bottom,
a spring, like that of a shot-belt, draws down
two guards, and likewise straightens the wire;
so that, whether the miner leaves his lamp alone
or meddles with it, it is impossible an explosion
can take place from it. In addition to this, Mr.
Ayre thinks it practicable to introduce, near the
flame, a piece of highly-polished tin, thus produc-
ing double the light by means of reflection. About
twelve months ago Mr. Ayre wrote to John Buddle,
Esq. (the principal viewer of our coal districts)
informing him of his invention, and solicited the
favour of being allowed to wait upon him at any
time or place most convenient. Mr. Ayre's letter,
however, did not receive common courtesy—and,
to the present time, has never been noticed by

Mr. Buddle. To the committee of the House of Commons, at present sitting to examine into the nature of coal mine explosions, Mr. Ayre has communicated his invention, and Mr. Pease, (one of the committee) has written to him, desiring that one might be sent to London immediately, which request has been complied with, and we hope the inventor will meet with a suitable reward. In conclusion we may add, that Professor Johnson, who was lately delivering some public lectures on chemistry in this town, waited upon Mr. Ayre, introduced the lamp in his lectures, and highly complimented him for the safety and ingenuity of his invention.

PUSHKIN PRESS—THE LONDON LIBRARY

"FOUND ON THE SHELVES"

THE LONDON LIBRARY (a registered charity) is one of the UK's leading literary institutions and a favourite haunt of authors, researchers and keen readers.

Membership is open to all.

Join at www.londonlibrary.co.uk.

www.pushkinpress.com